Published by Lift Bridge Publishing

Copyright © 2014 by Jabril Hasan

All Rights Reserved

Library of Congress Cataloging-in-Publication Data

Hasan, Jabril.

The Mind of Jabril Hasan: A Collection of Poems and Thoughts

ISBN 978-0-9961536-1-4

PRINTED IN THE UNITED STATES OF AMERICA

FIRST EDITION

Subconscious

What do you do when the one you've been waiting for STILL isn't ready? The way has been paved, and the example has been made. Much like history, you find yourself repeating. Repeating mistakes not made by you, but by your ancestral line in hopes of "correcting" the past. What do you do when the person you've been waiting for is you? Where do you start? How does one decide that this is the moment? That this is the moment to start anew. It's time to decide, are you gonna run and hide, or do you stand up and fight back with pride? No one needs this more than you. Fuck the chances you blew. Learn from them, they'll help you get through. Get up!! Something is waiting for you.

This book is dedicated to my people, my fellow (Colored, then Negro, then Black, and now) African-American people. May we begin to see our TRUE worth and, begin to live in that truth... I love you all.

The Mind Of Jabril Hasan:

A Collection of Poems and Thoughts

Walking In My Authority-

"I was wondering about our yesterdays and started digging through the rubble. To tell the truth somebody went through a hell of a lot of trouble. To make sure when we looked things up we wouldn't fare too well and come up with totally unreliable pictures of ourselves. But I've compiled what few facts I could. I mean, such as they are, to see if I could shed a little bit of light. This is what I've got so far…"

In 1619 we were brought here on ships not like the Titanic.

Then on January 1, 1863 massa began to panic.

For 244 years we were being exploited by not only the white man, but also by ourselves.

The house nigga after wippin' massa's ass was told to go whip the field nigga, for standin' up for himself.

That simple ass house nigga and his false sense of entitlement, not realizing that'll soon be him.

And as if that wasn't enough…

33 years later after our alleged freedom was handed to us, it was decided that "we best be seen where it wasn't so clean".

Just because THEY felt we "weren't good enough".

Who the fuck are y'all?

But that shit ain't last too long, cuz' 58 years later, things went from lesser than to greater when Linda Brown stood up and said "Fuck y'all!! I demand a better education!!"

Only to be righteously signed, sealed, & delivered by a man who had a dream 5 years later.

It was that same dream that laid the foundation for what became the hip-hop generation.

The Niggas

You know... Fuck the fact that people are walking around ignorant
as shit. Pants hangin' around their kneecaps, and the overall lack of
self-respect... Fuck the fact that our ancestors died fighting just so
we can call each other "nigga's" and "bitches", and your momma's
pussy needs stitches. You know... Fuck the fact that we as a people
will never live to our fullest potential because we refuse to accept the
fact that we are our biggest problem. The laziness that exists within
us will be our undertaking. So here's to ignorance. Here's to the
stupid motherfucker, and his friends... The Niggas

Daffodil: A Dedication To You

Through a man's mind he sees his elevation.

But through this man's mind he sees a limitation.

A Leo, and a Pisces, both tend to have egos as tall as redwood trees.

You've established your roots, often resting in the shade of your few fine branches.

You've made a name for yourself.

Managing to do what few people can…

Be your authentic self.

Cause see…

The signs of life are the signs of you.

All the elements it took to create you,

You access like a phone operator workin' a double-shift.

You're mellow.

You're cool.

You pity the fool.

But please don't be confused…

She'd take yo' ass to school!

See through a man's mind, he sees his elevation.

But through this man's mind, he sees a limitation.

I think it's time I moved on.

Better

At some point we have to give ourselves the "better" that we deserve.

Once blinded by my own pity, I would walk aimlessly through reality.

Not able to accept a compliment, my tongue became an exit ramp for my

false ego. Afraid of the feelings that my foundation needed to deal with, I

convinced myself that 'everyone else has problems'.

I held myself hostage, foreclosing on my own sanity.

My reality had become quicksand.

How fast my world has ended.

But still I stand.

Still I fight.

Eating to live.

Learning to forgive.

Piece by piece with new vision, new wisdom, and a new attitude.

(Ooh. Ooh. Ooh. Ooh. Ooh.)

(In the spirit of tomorrow) I introduce you to today.

Find a new way, and a say 'Okay, my new life begins today.' Everything will be okay.

What Ever Happened to HIP-HOP?

What ever happened to the original Hip-Hop?
The music that reflected the times
Celebrating the good
Surviving the bad
Now, Hip-Hop is remixed
Reflecting Rims, Killing snitches
Coppin Gold chains, and fuckin (bad) bitches
The world has gone flip flop without the original hip hop
No lyrics to soothe the soul when Michael Brown got shot
Not to mention...
Trayvon Martin.
Renisha McBride.
Eric Garner.
Darren Hunt.
Rekia Boyd.
Me?
You?
Will it ever end?
'Don't Push Me Cuz' I'm Close To The Edge'
Hip-Hop has truly lost its head.
Spittin lyrics about material wealth
'Versace! Versace! Versace! Versace! Versace!'
When in reality…
We dyin'! We dyin'! We dyin'! We dyin'! We dyin'!
So the question still stands…
What happened to Hip-Hop?

Hip-Hop would take ownership as the voice of the people.

Now it's nothing but counter-productive behavior, attitudes, and character.

The conscience has been lost.

The elements from which it was created have been re-formulated.

From the marginalized lives of (first Colored, then Negro, then Black) African-American.

To a form of self-repression.

Life is more than Jordans

Life is more than the money, and drugs that impair our minds

"Superstars and their love for the gain"...

(much love to Elle Maxwell)

Final Thought:

I have to give credit where credit is due

Yasiin Bey (formerly known as Mos Def)

Talib Kweli.

Lupe Fiasco.

Just to name a few…

You've saved my life

'Thank-You!!'

But to the rest of the Hip-Hop Generation

Ask yourselves,

"Am I contributing to the true essence of Hip-Hop?"

"Is it conducive to the education of my people?"

"Will a pair of 'Great & Powerful Jordans really help me feed my family?"

We need change.

"There's a revolution going on here in America.

A change as swift as blackening skies when the rain comes…"

(peace to Gil Scott-Heron)

It's time to rise up.

Now, more than ever.

It's time to revisit the true essence of hip –hop…

And save ourselves.

Just Be (In The Moment)

People Ask Me All the Time

"What You Wanna Be?"

I Tell Them

"I Just Wanna Be Me"

A Writer

A Teacher

A Fan in The Bleacher

Labels Tell Fables

Like Ann of Green Gables

Where People Dream Dreams

But Live in the Seams

The Seams of a Dream Deferred

Where Words Are Slurred

And Thoughts of a Better Life Fly Like a Bird

Why?

Cuz, That's The Word

I Am Time.

Like That Song Where the Song Is As Old As Rhyme

And Goes As Far As The Eye And Eye Can See.

That's All That's Needed from Me.

Like A Tree

I'm gnarled, but Content

There's No Need to Pay Rent

In The Kitchen, Too Much Time Was Spent

Digesting my emotions.

Nestle.

Nabisco.

"I'll Cook This With Crisco"

My Advice to You, Is to Be True To the First Person You Should've

Given Your Heart Too…

You.

(Honey) Let It Go.

Let It Flow

Simply Just….

Be.

Left. Right. Wrong. Write.

The Voices In My Head Sing Words That Have Yet To Be Said.

Like Songs From The Old Negro South Awaiting To Soar From My Mouth.

Like A Toucan Above The Canopy.

Don't You Know That You Can Be What You Wanna Be.

A Writer.

A Poet.

They're Almost The Same, Don't You Know It?

A Teacher.

A Preacher.

Or Simply A Fan In The Bleacher.

Cuz' See, In This Thing Called Life.

Despite The Pain, And the Trife.

Hidden In Disguise.

Often Right Before Our Eyes.

Is A Prize.

That To Me

Feels Like Sunrise.

Tastes Like A Plethora Of Pies.

And Is Tight Like That Thing Between Her Thighs.

And Yet, Of Course…

I Rise

Like The Rent In My Apartment.

Like The Roof At A Party Playing Parliament.

NOTICE: THIS BUS IS UNDER POLICE SURVELLANCE

Another Dead Black Kid Is The Alleged Assailant.

Emmitt Till.

Trayvon Martin.

Where's Their Movie Reel?

Or Shit, At Least A Milk Carton.

But We Ain't Supposed To Know.

We Damn Sho' And Supposed To See.

That For People Like You And Me.

That's How The Story Goes.

12 Years A Slave.

But 400 Years A Bitch Bad.

Just Like The Turnpike…

The Bell Tolls.

Let It Flow

"See the thing of it is we deserve respect. But we can't demand respect without change."

Self-absorbed.

Lost within a lost world.

Jurassic like tendencies reveal a life lived on repeat.

Actin' a fool.

Doin' nothing with himself.

Blessings become curses.

His words are sand castles washed away by the tide.

Pride.

That virtue, but more often a vice clearly comes with a high price.

Every morning...

New disguises are his personal prizes.

"Who shall I be today?"

"How shall I act?"

Going out of his way to hear people say

"Oh, you're so wonderful!!"

But is he really?

He preaches being your 'Authentic Self'

But he forgot to take his own advice.

Everyday he sells another slice.

Another slice of himself, while the rest of him stays on dry ice.

Waiting for Bob Barker, or Drew Carey to tell him his 'Price Is Right'.

What a life.

What a plight.

When you start to lose sight.

Ask yourself:

Am I being my Authentic(best) Self?

Or am I feeding into the false egos of other people?

Letting Go

Letting go is always the hardest part.

Saying goodbye to my ego.

Saying Goodbye to co-dependency.

Waving toodles to the oodles, and oodles of of lonely nights, and hope-
less

days.

To the "No, I'm not mad" 's, and "No, that's okay" 's.

I'm waving goodbye to the 'Bad Ole' Days'.

And saying hello to the new ways.

The new ways of thinking.

And new ways of being.

I'm tired of being tired.

Tired of being that street car I once desired.

Offering a free ride on my shaky pride.

Well guess what...?!

That person has died!!

(Waves) Goodbye!!

(I'm From The) Old School

Verse 1

Well, I woke up this mornin',

(Just as) Sad as can be.

My momma dead

And my cat left me.

My baby gone (Awwww Lawwwd!!)

I'm (in this world) all alone

I don't know what to

'Cept drink a bottle or two.

Hook

I'm from the old school!!

That's how we did it back then (yeah, yeah!!)

I sho' ain't no fool

I'm from the old school!!

Verse 2

I've got a GED and an Associate's Degree.

I work at KFC

That job so crappy

It sucks the life out of me

I'm just as blue as can be

Got to hit this loud pack

And get my back on track.

Guitar Solo

Hook

I'm from the old school!!

That's how we did it back then (yeah, yeah!!)

I sho' ain't no fool

I'm from the old school!!

Rebirth: A Second Dedication

Through a man's mind he sees his elevation.

But through this man's mind, he sees a limitation.

The naive side of me wonders what I do to not get "enough" attention from you.

The mature side of me says "She's Human Too"

Lessons are blessins' that make fountains out of mountains.

Universal truths show me sides of you that make me question myself.

Allowing me to chuckle as I look back over my life.

I've come a long assistance way.

Especially when I accepted my being gay.

"Too many sheep wanna chief with the beast." (Peace to Elle Maxwell)

But as time moves on.

So do I.

*Daffodils are a symbol of Rebirth and/or new beginnings. Tides carry away the prides of a once naive person. Allowing him to start again.

Time Machine

Through a man's mind he sees his elevation.

But through this man's mind he sees a limitation.

Wandering.

Searching.

Looking for a place to fit in.

Hoping for a chance to start again.

See, years ago, I lost sight of myself in the vision of others.

Often finding myself sleeping in the mirror, I make broken promises

To myself that "tomorrow I'll start fresh".

"Tomorrow, I'll begin again".

Stuck in the caboose

on the train of life.

'Shoulda, coulda, woulda's' fill my lungs like smog from a loud pack.

If only I could go back.

Back to the times when we lived without lights.

Back to the days when we they took our water, but you said 'that's alright!!'

See you had no foundation, no 'Shining Time Station'.

With dreams of living Eureka's castle, reality was always a hassle.

No one showed you how to make a $1.oo out of $0.15.

How long did you think they'd notice, you hadn't paid the rent?

"This is Robin Leech here, with Lifestyles of The Rich & Famous".

He called Freddie Mac and shamed us.

Stevey went it' her girlfriend.

Frank went to prison

I moved in with my dad.

But that wasn't the best decision.

They foreclosed on the house; you foreclosed on your emotions.

You got caught up in the sorrow; I'll have to finish this tomorrow.

Travelin'

In order to know where you're going...

You have to know where you've been.

But to know where you've been...

It helps to know who your parents were.

A mother of two until you met dog number two.

Promised yourself after the first romance

You wouldn't give love a second chance.

Along came Ahmad as he did his little dance.

He said "I'll be there for ya".

"Together we can make things right."

Little did she know

He would be added stress to her pain and plight.

Then somewhere between May and June.

Underneath a blue moon...

She found herself conceiving another child too soon.

They say that "Spring Can Really Hang You Up..."

But what about the bummer of Summer?

The long days, and the strong sun rays.

Penny Candy, and a house that ain't that damn dandy.

He (Ahmad) left for four years.

The first of many.

You said "That's Alright!!"

Frank, Stevey, and Jabril.

Let me take a sip of water, before I give the real deal.

Thoughts Of A Black Man Scorned

We've witnessed our people swing from the trees of social injustice.
We've witnessed our people brutally beat down due to the political
inequality of democracy. We've witnessed the destruction of
our people as they chose to stand for their beliefs as humans and
their rights as American citizens. Regardless of circumstances they
walked with dignity and determination. Now it is our turn. It is
time to get back in line and walk in their footsteps toward change.
Unfortunately these classifications have divided black America. We
have to ban together in order to enforce change. No more crabs
in a basket mentality, and rejecting our heritage due to embarrass-
ment.

When we fight for our life, we fight for the life of our
brothers. Blinded by instant gratification of material objects,we
have lost sight of our purpose, and our destiny. Disillusioned by
music videos, movies, and reality t.v., we are driven by a false sense
of security and a false sense of what it means to live. Guess who is
playing the part of the puppet and guess who is pulling the strings.
Cash is ruling everything around us and our future and the future
of our generation is being destroyed.

Black America is in need of a social resurrection. We have to be
raised up from the dead,and walk with vitality; a renewed sense
of self and ability. The only limitations we have are what we put
on ourselves. Whether we stand alone or in unity, we must stand.
Stand on the shoulders of our ancestors who were forcefully
brought over on slave ships. Stand on the shoulders of our ancestors
who had to enter hotels and movie theatres through the back door.

Stand on the shoulders of our ancestors who fought and died for us with hope of their children being free. This time we shall stand without wavering and uncertainty so the next generation can stand on our shoulders and proclaim, "Yes!! I'm black, and proud!! I'm black, and beautiful!!"

Our freedom came with a cost. The Emancipation Proclamation did not save us; we've had to make provisions for ourselves. There is no better time than now to believe in the person you were created to be and believe in what you were created to do. Walk boldly and upright in your self-proclaimed freedom. When you believe in yourself, and have faith, no one can take that away from you.

Embrace your heritage and be proud of the solid foundation that has been laid out for you. We've gotten this far by faith and with this same faith we can and must go further.

Notes on:

Daffodil: A Dedication To You

&

Rebirth: A Second Dedication

These two poems are dedicated to Dappho The Flow-Er of The Coo-Lots.

The CooLots are the original Rock/Soul band hailing from the Washington, DC area. A melting pot of different styles and talents, The CooLots come together to create feelings never experienced before. These creations embody sincerity, musicality, rock, funk, and soul, with influences including: N.E.R.D, Me'Shell N'Degeocello, Sade, Staind, Erykah Badu, Kanye West and System of A Down. You can hear all these influences on The CooLots EP - their debut effort, released January 7th, 2014.

To Dappho-

You are my teacher, and my friend. I thank-you for the lessons, the laughs, and the occasional beverage. You make me so damn happy. XOXOXOXOXOXO

Notes On:

Whatever Happened To Hip-Hop?

Elle Maxwell is mentioned twice once here (secondly in Rebirth: A Second Dedication). Elle Maxwell is a multi-media artist native to Washington, DC. She is the founder and designer of/at The Regal People, LLC, as well as a rapper under the name Miss Jillz, Lola Maxwell, and Elle Maxwell (present) since 2007.

To Ms. Elle Maxwell- I remember the day we met, and I thank-you for the breath of fresh air. My only wish is for you to continue to shine your light on the world. XOXOXOXO

www.ingramcontent.com/pod-product-compliance
Lightning Source LLC
Chambersburg PA
CBHW060623070426
42449CB00042B/2482